Canadian Cookbook

Delicious Canadian Recipes that will Offer you a Taste of Canada

Table of Contents

Introduction 4

    Lobster Poutine 6

    Canadian Goose Bacon Skewers 8

    Nanaimo Bars 10

    Maple Crème Brûlée with Hazelnuts 13

    Sugar Pie 16

    Pork Ball Stew 18

    Canadian Moose Lasagna 20

    Canadian Goose with Dark Sweet Cherries 23

    Classic Rabbit Stew 26

    French Canadian Venison Tourtiere 29

    Fish and Brewis 32

    Salt Cod Cakes 34

    Teriyaki Salmon 37

    Goose Sausage 39

    Fish Stew 42

    Canadian Burger with Beer Braised Onions and Cheddar .. 45

    Nori Crusted Salmon 48

    Maple Syrup Upside-Down Cake 51

    Cedar Planked Salmon 53

    Foie Gras Poutine 55

    Red Velvet, Jos Louis Cake 58

Lobster Macaroni and Cheese 61

Veal and Roquefort Poutine 64

Ketchup Chip Snack 67

Garlic Fingers with Donair Sauce 69

Maple Sundae 72

Canadian Bacon and Vegetable Soup 74

Canadian Fried Dough Treat 76

Canadian Bacon with Maple Syrup 79

Maple Fennel Bacon 81

Conclusion 83

Introduction

Good Canadian food will always be enjoyed and liked. Recipes such as Maple Crème Brûlée, with hazelnuts, Sugar pie and French-Canadian Venison Tourtiere are some of the fabulous dishes you will learn to prepare from this cookbook.

Some national foods of Canada are, poutine, Montreal-style bagels, dried smoked salmon, maple syrup, butter tarts. These ingredients combined with others can create a healthy balanced meal. This cookbook will teach you all about it and will also teach you a simple style of Canadian cooking which will produce some very tasty and delicious meals.

Canadian food is easy to enjoy and remember, real Canadian Cuisine is a combination of many interesting cuisines and this cookbook will teach you and assist you in preparing same. Don't miss out on this great opportunity, grab your copy today!

Lobster Poutine

A classic Canadian dish which will blow your taste buds away and leave your guests craving for more.

Serves: 4

Time: 25 minutes

Ingredients:

- 1 teaspoon salt
- ½ cup butter
- 1 tablespoon cornstarch
- 2 cups cooked lobster meat

- 8 slices bread
- ¼ teaspoon ground black pepper
- 2 tablespoons butter or as needed
- 2 cups light cream, divided

Directions:

1. Dissolve ½ cup butter in a skillet, once hot add the lobster and heat through for 5 minutes, then season.

2. Beat 1 tablespoon of cream together with the cornstarch in a bowl.

3. Add the rest of the cream to the lobster, now mix in the cream with the cornstarch and cook for 5 minutes until it becomes thick.

4. Place the bread in the toaster and smear over the 2 tablespoons butter when done.

5. Spoon the lobster onto 1 slice of toast. Cover with another slice, then spoon another lobster over the top. Serve.

Canadian Goose Bacon Skewers

This will be enjoyed by your family and friends and quite easy to prepare. Doubt there will be any leftovers.

Serves: 6

Time: 1 hour and 5 minutes

Ingredients:

- 1 pack McCormick grill mates, southwest
- 6 goose breasts
- 6 – ½ inch thick rasher Canadian bacon
- 1 bottle Soy Teriyaki sauce

- Barbeque sauce (if desired)

Directions:

1. Dice the goose breast into 1 ½ inch pieces with the skin removed.

2. Place half of the meat into the teriyaki sauce and the other half in the mate's powder, place both in the fridge for 30 minutes to marinate.

3. While waiting heat the barbeque and grease the bars.

4. Meanwhile, slice the bacon into 1 ½ inch pieces.

5. Place both meats on the skewer alternating them. Once the skewers are full, place on the grill to cook.

6. Flip over while cooking, be sure not to overcook the meat.

7. Dish up with your choice of sauce to finish and enjoy while hot.

Nanaimo Bars

A quick and easy delicious homemade dessert. It's a rich semi-sweet chocolate bar with a flaked coconut and creamy custard.

Serves: 18

Time: 2 hours and 30 minutes

Ingredients:

For the crust:

- ½ teaspoon salt

- 1 cup graham cracker crumbs
- 1 cup unsweetened flaked coconut
- 3 tablespoons cocoa powder
- 1 large egg, beaten lightly
- 6 tablespoons unsalted butter (melted)
- ½ cup walnut pieces

For the filling:

- 2 tablespoons vanilla custard powder
- ½ cup unsalted butter (softened)
- 3 tablespoons milk
- 2 cups icing sugar (sifted)
- 1 teaspoon vanilla extract
- Pinch salt

For the topping:

- 2 tablespoon unsalted butter
- 4 ounces' semisweet chocolate (chopped)
- Sea salt for dusting (if desired)

Directions:

1. Heat the stove to 350 degrees F and grease an 8×8-inch pan, then place parchment paper inside and up the sides.

2. Blend together the cocoa, salt and crumbs in a bowl and then put in the walnut and coconut pieces.

3. Now stir in the butter with the egg and mix together thoroughly.

4. Place the mix in the pan and compress it evenly, cook in the oven for 12 minutes, then remove and cool.

5. While it is cooling, whisk together 1 cup icing sugar, butter and custard powder, add a pinch of salt.

6. Once it becomes smooth mix in the vanilla and milk, whisk again, mix in the rest of the icing sugar.

7. Place the mix over the base of the crust and even out.

8. Next, place a pot of water to heat, using a bowl that sits on top of the pot, add the chocolate with the butter and stir them together over the steam.

9. When ready smear the chocolate over the top of the filling, and dust with salt if desired.

10. Place the bars in the fridge and chill for a minimum of 2 hours before cutting into fingers.

Maple Crème Brûlée with Hazelnuts

A rich creamy maple custard, nicely contrasted by a crunchy caramelized sugar topping. Perfect for entertaining.

Serves: 6

Time: 1 hour and 5 minutes

Ingredients:

- 3 tablespoons sugar
- Cooking spray

- ⅓ cup pure maple syrup
- 2 cups whipping cream
- 6 egg yolks
- ¼ cup sugar
- ¼ cup chopped hazelnuts or almonds, toasted
- ⅛ teaspoon salt
- 1 ½ teaspoons vanilla

Directions:

1. Heat the stove to 350 degrees F, and grease 6 ramekins, using the cooking spray.

2. Put the ramekins into a baking dish and keep on the side.

3. Add 3 tablespoons of sugar and the whipping cream to a heavy based pan and heat, stir as you heat, as it starts bubbling, remove from heat and set aside.

4. Next, blend together the vanilla, egg yolks, salt and syrup in a bowl, whisk together until thoroughly blended.

5. Now gently add the hot cream, then pour the mix into the ramekins.

6. Add water to the dish filling it halfway up the side of the ramekins.

7. Cook in the oven for 35 minutes or until they have set.

8. Take out and place on a cooling rack. Once cooled, place in the refrigerator for 60 minutes.

9. When ready to serve, remove from the refrigerator 30 minutes before.

10. Now, prepare the caramel, using an 8-inch skillet add ¼ cup sugar and heat, as it melts shake and cook for around 5 minutes until it changes to a golden color. Drizzle over the top of the ramekins.

11. Dust with the nuts and serve.

Sugar Pie

A traditional dessert for the Canadian province of Quebec. A very popular pie with a nice flaky crust and a rich caramel custard filling.

Serves: 2

Time: 55 minutes

Ingredients:

- 1 cup light whipping cream
- 2 cups brown sugar
- 1 cup milk
- 1 tablespoon flour
- ½ teaspoon vanilla

- 1 prepared pie crust

Directions:

1. Blend together the flour with the sugar, now mix in the cream, butter, vanilla and milk.

2. Place the mix in a pan and simmer until it starts to thicken. While waiting, stir the mix to prevent it from burning.

3. Heat the stove to 350 degrees F.

4. Add the pie crust to a pie plate then add the filling.

5. Cook in the oven for 40 minutes or until it sets.

6. Take out when ready, slice and serve.

Pork Ball Stew

A healthy stew using homemade meatballs. The perfect dish on a cold Winter night.

Serves: 6-8

Time: 1 hour and 45 minutes

Ingredients:

- 1 teaspoon salt
- 2 pounds lean ground pork
- 1 egg

- 1 medium onion, chopped fine
- ½ teaspoon pepper

Herbs for seasoning:

- 2 cups hot water or bouillon
- 3-4 tablespoons of breadcrumbs
- Oil for cooking

Directions:

1. Place the meat in a bowl and blend together with the seasoning and herbs, add the onion and mix well.

2. Next put in the egg and add some breadcrumbs to achieve a solid but not too dry mix.

3. Mold the mix into balls. Grease a skillet and put to heat.

4. Once hot, seal the balls all over and remove any excess fat from the skillet.

5. Now add the bouillon or water to the skillet and simmer for 1 ½ hours.

6. Thicken the sauce using the flour, then serve.

Canadian Moose Lasagna

A traditional Italian dish. This cheesy moose lasagna recipe can be served with garlic bread and a salad.

Serves: 4

Time: 1 hour and 35 minutes

Ingredients:

- 2 clove garlic (minced)
- 2 tablespoons olive oil
- 4 mushrooms (sliced)
- 1 onion (minced)
- 1-pound ground moose

- spinach (1 bunch, washed and chopped)
- ½ teaspoon brown sugar
- ricotta cheese (1 jar-16 ounce)
- 1 – 24-ounce jar spaghetti sauce
- cocoa powder (1/2 tsp., unsweetened)
- 1 tablespoon Italian seasoning
- ¾ cup water
- 1 ½ cups shredded mozzarella cheese

Seasoning to taste:

- ¼ cup parmesan cheese (grated)
- 1 tablespoon dried oregano
- 1 – 9 ounces pack no boil lasagna noodles

Directions:

1. Heat the stove to 350 degrees F and grease a 9×13-inch-deep sided tray.

2. Now add oil to a skillet and heat. Once hot, fry the garlic with the onions until they become soft, roughly 5-7 minutes.

3. Drop in the mushrooms and cook for a further 3 minutes, remove from heat.

4. Next, put on a pan with ⅓ cup of salted water, add the spinach and cook until wilted. Strain off the water and blend together with the onion mix, stir in the ricotta cheese.

5. Using a separate skillet cook the moose meat until it is no longer pink in color, then add the sugar and cocoa, blend together well.

6. Once cooked, remove any excess fat and mix in the spaghetti sauce, oregano, seasoning, Italian seasoning and water.

7. When properly mixed, add a ladle full of the meat to the tray, then add a layer of the noodles, then a layer of the cheese mix followed by the tomato sauce and parmesan.

8. Add some mozzarella, then repeat the process.

9. Finish with a good covering of the mozzarella, place foil over the top and cook in the oven for 45 minutes.

10. Serve when bubbly and hot.

Canadian Goose with Dark Sweet Cherries

This recipe can be used with any choice of geese. Perfectly complimented with the sweet cherry sauce.

Serves: 4

Time: 4 hours and 25 minutes

Ingredients:

- 2 tablespoons butter
- 1 Canada goose, skin on or off
- 1 large onion, diced

- 2 – 16-ounce cans pitted dark sweet cherries
- 2 tablespoons all-purpose flour
- 2 tablespoon vegetable oil
- 2 tablespoons brown sugar
- ½ teaspoon salt
- 3 tablespoons brandy or cognac
- 2 teaspoons beef base
- 2 tablespoons water
- 1 teaspoon ground cinnamon
- 2 tablespoon cornstarch

Directions:

1. Cut the goose in half down the center, then take out the back bone. Next, cut the two halves in two, giving you 4 pieces, then place them on the side.

2. Strain the cherries and keep 1 cup of the juice aside.

3. Place the oil and butter in a Dutch oven and once hot fry the onions for 5-7 minutes.

4. Place the 4 pieces of goose in and seal all over, until golden, then remove and put aside.

5. Blend in the flour with the onion, add the sugar, beef base, salt, cherry juice, brandy and cinnamon, stir together until it becomes thick.

6. Heat the stove to 325 degrees F.

7. Place the goose back in and cook in the oven for 3 ½ hours with a lid on.

8. When ready transfer the goose to the serving dish and keep warm.

9. If the sauce needs to be thickened, use the water and cornstarch to thicken over a medium heat.

10. Once thickened, serve the gravy over the goose.

Classic Rabbit Stew

A simple Ontario Rabbit stew with homestyle flavors of carrots, tomatoes and onions combined with the Ontario rabbit.

Serves: 4-6

Time: 1 hour and 55 minutes

Ingredients:

- 2 tablespoons extra virgin olive oil
- 1 – 3 ½ pound Ontario rabbit, cut into 8 sections
- 2 onions (sliced)

- 1 teaspoon salt
- 1 teaspoon pepper
- 1 celery stalk (sliced)
- 2 carrots (peeled and sliced)
- 1 cup dry red wine
- 1 bay leaf
- 2 cloves garlic (chopped fine)
- ½ pound dried broad egg noodles
- 1 tablespoon chopped flat leaf parsley
- 1 – 28 ounce can whole tomatoes

Directions:

1. Place a large skillet with oil to heat.

2. In the meantime, dry the rabbit and season with ½ teaspoon of pepper and salt.

3. Cooking in two batches seal the rabbit until golden, all over roughly 6 minutes per batch.

4. Remove from skillet and keep on the side when done. Lower the heat under the skillet and sauté the celery, onion and carrots for 5 minutes.

5. Next, add the garlic and after 1 minute add the wine, this will help remove the sediments from the sides and base of the skillet.

6. Heat the stove to 350 degrees F.

7. Now add the tomatoes, the rest of the seasoning and bay leaf to the skillet, lay the rabbit pieces in and simmer.

8. Place tin foil over the top and cook in the middle of the oven for 30 minutes, flip over the rabbit and cook for another 30 minutes.

9. While the rabbit is being cooked, cook the noodles in salted boiling water.

10. When ready strain off the water and place on the serving platters.

11. Place the rabbit over the noodles and pour sauce over the rabbit, finish with the parsley.

French Canadian Venison Tourtiere

A traditional Christmas dish for many French- Canadian families. A meat pie tender and cozy enough to be served on a cold Winter's night accompanied with a bottle of champagne.

Serves: 6-8

Time: 1 hour and 15 minutes

Ingredients:

- ½ pound ground venison
- 1 clove garlic, crushed and chopped fine
- Pate Brisee or store pastry dough for a double crust

- ½ pound ground pork
- ¾ cup diced onion
- ¼ cup finely chopped celery
- ⅓ cup grated carrots
- 1 tablespoon cognac
- ⅔ cup beef stock
- ¾ cup small potatoes, diced
- ¾ teaspoon salt
- ¼ teaspoon ground black pepper
- 1 teaspoon dried parsley
- ¼ teaspoon dried sage
- Pinch grated nutmeg
- Pinch ground cloves
- 1 tablespoon dry breadcrumbs
- Pinch ground allspice
- ½ cup mashed potatoes, seasoned

Directions:

1. Heat the stove to 400 degrees F.

2. Divide the pastry into 2 pieces. Roll them out to the same size rounds to fit on a pie plate. and set aside.

3. Next, put on a skillet to heat with oil, once hot fry the onion, pork, carrots, venison, potatoes and celery, until the meat is cooked.

4. Pour off the excess fat, then pour in the cognac, stock, add the spices and herbs stir together and cook simmering for 20 minutes.

5. When ready take the skillet off the heat and mix in the breadcrumbs and potatoes now rest for 3-4 minutes.

6. Take the pie plate lay the pastry over it and spoon in the meat mix, lay the second pastry round over the top.

7. Seal the edges well, crimping them together and add 2-3 cuts in the top to allow the steam to escape.

8. Place in the oven and cook for 10 minutes, then turn down the heat to 350 degrees F and cook for a further 30 minutes.

9. Once golden take out, cool for 5 minutes, slice and serve.

Fish and Brewis

A traditional Newfoundland dish consisting of cooked salt cod and soaked hard bread.

Serves: 6-8

Time: 55 minutes

Ingredients:

- 1 cup salt pork
- 2 pounds' salt cod
- 6 loaves hard bread, Canadian hard biscuit

Directions:

1. Soak fish in a pan covered with water overnight.

2. Do the same with the hard bread, overnight.

3. When ready, strain off the water from the fish, return to the pan and cover with fresh water.

4. Heat over medium-high flame until it starts simmering, cover and cook for 20 minutes.

5. Once cooked, strain off the water and break the fish into the serving size. Set aside.

6. Place the container with the soaked hard bread over medium-flame. Once it simmers cook for 15 minutes with a lid on.

7. When it's done strain off the water. Divide among serving platters. Add the fish.

8. Place the platters in a low oven to keep warm.

9. Cut the pork into small pieces and fry in a skillet. Once golden brown, place on top of the fish and bread.

10. Serve and enjoy.

Salt Cod Cakes

These Salt Cod cakes are very tasty, quick and easy to prepare. Great choice for breakfast.

Serves: 16

Time: 55 minutes

Ingredients:

- ½ pound thick cut smoked bacon, diced
- 1-pound boneless salt cod fillets
- 1 teaspoon black pepper
- 4 pounds' russet potatoes, peeled and quartered

- 1 tablespoon vegetable oil, for frying
- 1 onion, diced
- 2 teaspoon summer savory

Directions:

1. Wash the fish to remove the excess salt.

2. Add 8 cups of water to a bowl or dish and put in the fish, leave overnight in the refrigerator.

3. When ready to cook, strain off the water from the fish, and add to a large pot with the potatoes, pour in water until it reaches roughly 4 inches above the ingredients.

4. Bring to a boil, then let simmer for roughly 35 minutes or until the potatoes are cooked.

5. While waiting fry the bacon in a skillet for 2 minutes, next add the peppers and onion with the summer savory. Fry for 7-8 minutes crisping the bacon around the edge.

6. Remove from heat and place on the side, leave in the fat.

7. Remove the water from the fish and potatoes leaving them in the pot.

8. Now, add the bacon mix including the fat and mash together, using a potato masher, leaving it chunky, cool on the side.

9. Once cooled down, enough to handle, mold into patties, place cling-wrap over and chill for 20 minutes in the refrigerator.

10. Add the oil to a skillet and cook the patties until golden brown and heated through, flipping them over halfway.

11. Serve.

Teriyaki Salmon

A sure winner! Simple ingredients, no lengthy marinating, simply delicious. Perfect for a weeknight supper.

Serves: 4-6

Time: 25 minutes

Ingredients:

- ⅓ cup soy sauce
- ¼ cup butter
- 8 cloves garlic, chopped

- ⅓ cup liquid honey
- 1 ½ pounds salmon meat
- 2 tablespoons fresh grated ginger

Directions:

1. Place the honey, garlic, butter, ginger and soy into a heavy based pan and heat until it becomes thick.

2. Lay in the salmon, flipping over as it cooks.

3. Once the salmon flakes take off the heat and serve.

Goose Sausage

A sizzling dish for your backyard barbecue or your stovetop in your kitchen. Whichever the method, they are still very tasty.

Serves: 6

Time: 60 minutes

Ingredients

- ½ teaspoon fennel seeds
- 4 goose breasts, skin off
- ½ teaspoon fennel powder

- ½ pound ground sausage
- ½ teaspoon garlic powder
- ½ teaspoon ginger powder
- ½ teaspoon kosher salt

Directions

1. Place the goose in the freezer 30 minutes before making them, making it easier to cut.

2. When ready to prepare, remove from the freezer and slice into ¾ inch cubes.

3. Place the meat either into a grinder or a blender, and pulse until it becomes fine.

4. Keep pushing the meat down in between pulsing.

5. Once ready take out and place into a bowl, now add the rest of the ingredients and it together well using your hands.

6. Mold into ½ thick round patties.

7. Add 1 tablespoon oil to a skillet and heat, lay in the patties and cook for 7 minutes then flip over and cook for another 7 minutes, this can be done in batches.

8. Serve with your desired vegetables or even in a burger bun.

Fish Stew

A quick and simple one-pot meal. Great family meal and absolutely delicious!

Serves: 2

Time: 65 minutes

Ingredients

- 3 tablespoons vegetable oil
- 1 large fish head (cleaned, cod is a good choice)

- 2 bay leaves
- 1 tablespoon turmeric (divided)
- 2 red sun-dried chilies
- Pinch salt
- Pinch cumin powder
- Pinch pepper
- Pinch phoron, can be got in Asian or specialty store
- 1 small stick cinnamon stick
- 2 cloves garlic, chopped
- 1 ½ large onion, diced fine
- 1 ½ cups boiled water
- ½ tomato, chopped
- Pinch chili powder
- ½ cup dried lentils (soaked and cooked as per instructions on the packet)
- 1 lemon, juiced
- Cooked rice (brown or basmati)
- Fresh coriander leaves

Directions

1. Blend together ½ tablespoon turmeric and seasoning, smear and rub into the fish head and leave on the side for 10 minutes.

2. Heat a pan with 1 tablespoon of oil and drop in the fish head, fry on either side for 10 minutes.

3. Once golden-brown remove from heat and use a spoon break it apart, then set it aside.

4. Using another pan, add a little oil and heat. Add cumin, cinnamon stick, 2 pinches of phoron, bay leaves and chilies, fry for 4-6 minutes.

5. Next, add the onions and stir together for an additional 5 minutes.

6. Put in the garlic and cook for a further 5 minutes. Finally, add the chili powder and leftover turmeric and cook until it becomes dry, roughly 5 minutes more.

7. Stir in the fish head and the boiling water. Now add the lentils and simmer for 15 minutes.

8. Pour in the lemon juice and tomatoes for the final 12 minutes of cooking.

9. Finish with coriander and serve with rice.

Canadian Burger with Beer Braised Onions and Cheddar

A classic Canadian burger with a hint of beer.

Serves: 4

Time: 35 minutes

Ingredients

- 1 tablespoon sugar
- 1 tablespoon butter
- 1 ½ pounds fresh ground beef or ground round
- 1 large onion, sliced thin

- ¾ cup Canadian beer
- 2 cloves garlic, minced
- 2 tablespoons Dijon mustard
- ¼ cup finely diced red pepper
- 2 cups grated cheddar cheese
- ¼ cup Canadian beer
- 4 burger buns
- Seasoning to taste

Directions

1. Place the butter in a skillet over medium flame and heat.

2. Once dissolved add the onions and fry for 5-7 minutes, stirring frequently.

3. Add the ¾ cup of beer along with the sugar, fry until the dissolves and the onions have change to a nice golden color, roughly 15 minutes.

4. Meanwhile heat the grill and grease the bars.

5. Place the meat, ¼ cup of beer, seasoning, red pepper, garlic and mustard in a bowl and blend it all together.

6. Mold into 1-inch thick burgers and cook on the grill for 5 minutes either side.

7. Place ½ of cheese on each burger and cook until it dissolves.

8. Place on top of toasted buns finishing with the onions over the top.

Nori Crusted Salmon

A nutritious crusted salmon flavored with natural herbs. A delicious protein dish!

Serves: 4

Time: 40 minutes

Ingredients

For the crust

- 1 ½ tablespoons sesame seeds
- 2 nori sheets, toasted
- 2 tablespoons butter

- 1 teaspoon paprika
- 1 teaspoon black peppercorns
- 1 Thai chili, sliced
- 1 shallot, minced
- 1 clove garlic, minced
- Salt to taste

For the salmon

- 1 tablespoon butter
- 1 teaspoon vegetable oil
- 4 – 5-6-ounce salmon fillets, skin off
- Salt
- Nori crust

Directions

1. Break the toasted nori sheets using a mortar and pestle.

2. Put in the sesame seeds, salt, paprika and peppercorns and grind again.

3. Add the butter to a small pan and heat until dissolved.

4. Drop in the garlic with the shallots and fry for 3-5 minutes.

5. Next, put in the nori mix and the chili, stir together for 2 minutes and then remove from the heat.

6. Heat the stove to 350 degrees F.

7. Prepare a pan with the butter and oil and heat.

8. Rub the fillets of fish with seasoning on both sides and seal in the pan, flipping over after 2 minutes.

9. Take the fillets out and lay in a baking tray with the skin side down.

10. Then, add the nori mix to the top and compress slightly.

11. Cook in the oven for 6 minutes. Once it is cooked through take out and serve.

Maple Syrup Upside-Down Cake

One of the best upside-down cake recipe ever with the maple syrup infusing both the apple and the cake.

Serves: 16

Time: 1 hour

Ingredients

- sugar (3 tablespoons)
- 1 cup maple syrup
- 1 egg
- 1 tablespoon butter, softened
- flour (1 cup)
- salt (pinch)

- ½ cup milk
- 2 teaspoons baking powder
- ¼ teaspoon cinnamon
- Vanilla ice cream for serving:
- ¼ cup chopped walnuts

Directions

1. Heat the stove to 350 degrees F.

2. Add the egg, butter and sugar to a bowl and beat together until it becomes creamy.

3. Mix the salt, baking powder, cinnamon and flour together in a separate bowl.

4. Now, mix the dry mix into the wet mix slowly adding the milk at the same time alternating them as you mix them in.

5. Grease an 8-inch square baking dish. Bring the syrup to a boil, then pour it into the baking dish, sprinkle the nuts over evenly.

6. Section the dough into 4 and place in the syrup, using 2 forks, pull the dough to fit the dish.

7. Cook for 30 minutes. Serve with ice cream.

Cedar Planked Salmon

A tasty, inexpensive recipe. A mainstay on restaurant menus but can be prepared from your very own kitchen.

Serves: 2

Time: 1 hour 5 minutes

Ingredients:

- 1 thin lemon slice for each fillet, cut in two
- 2 salmon filets, 2 inches wide with the skin
- 2 thin slices red onion, cut in two
- 2 cloves garlic, minced

- 2 tablespoons dill, chopped fine
- ¼ cup fresh dill
- Ground black pepper to taste

Directions:

1. Take the cedar plank and soak as per the package directions, if there are none, a thin plank takes around 30 minutes, the thicker the longer.

2. Heat the outside grill at least 15 minutes before using, to get hot.

3. Add the planks to the grill and cover to allow them to smoke, this normally takes about 15 minutes.

4. Meanwhile, lay the salmon out on a platter with the skin down and place the lemon, chopped dill, garlic, onion and pepper over the top.

5. When the cedar is ready, transfer the salmon to the planks, cover and cook for 20 minutes.

6. Once it flakes easy, check the middle with a knife to see it is hot.

7. Serve while still juicy and not dry.

Foie Gras Poutine

A very popular dish in Montreal. Also, a creative vegetarian dish.

Serves: 4

Time: 17 minutes

Ingredients:

For the sauce:

- PDC poutine sauce (2 ½ cups)
- 7 ounces fresh foie gras
- ¼ cup cream

- 6 egg yolks

Foie gras and presentation:

- 4 white potatoes (cut into French fries)
- 4 – 3 ½ ounce slices foie gras (1 inch thick, fresh)
- Oil for frying:
- 14 ounces' cheese curds

Directions:

1. Reserve half cup of the sauce for serving.

2. Boil the poutine sauce in a pan.

3. While waiting add the cream, egg yolks and foie gras to the blender and pulse.

4. Once the poutine sauce is hot, carefully add 2 cups of this to the blender, pulsing in slowly.

5. Return it to a pan and heat to 175 degrees F, then remove from heat and mix for 30 seconds. then keep warm.

6. Heat the stove to 450 degrees F.

7. Take the sliced foie gras and add to a hot pan to color, when golden brown, remove and place them on a baking tray.

8. Cook in the oven for 4 minutes.

9. Meanwhile, cook the French fries until they become crispy, once ready place them on the cheese curds in the middle of the platter.

10. Add a slice of the seared foie over the top of the fries, then pour over the sauce.

11. Serve hot.

Red Velvet, Jos Louis Cake

An exotic desert and a portable lunch box favorite.

Serves: 12

Time: 1 hour 30 minutes

Ingredients:

- 1 ½ cups icing sugar
- 1 box red velvet cake mix (baked in 2# 9-inch pans as per instructions)
- whipping cream (1/2 cup)
- 2 jars marshmallow crème

- ½ cup unsalted butter
- ⅓ cup whipping cream, for the glaze
- 1⅓ cups chocolate chips

Directions:

1. Take one of the cooked sponges and slice the rounded top off, place on a platter.

2. Let the second sponge remain as is.

3. Next, make the whipping cream. When it peaks, beat in the icing sugar and butter for 2-3 minutes, until it becomes stiff.

4. Gently stir in the marshmallows.

5. Evenly smear the mix over the sponge on the platter, then add the other sponge on top.

6. Put the cake into the freezer for 10 minutes to chill.

7. Meanwhile, place the chocolate chip and cream in the microwave for 30 seconds to dissolve.

8. Stir the two together and allow to cool slightly.

9. Take out the cake and smear the glaze over the top and around the sides.

10. Place in the fridge for 60 minutes.

11. When ready take out and slice into 12 wedges.

Lobster Macaroni and Cheese

A rich macaroni and cheese dish enriched with zesty cheese. A quick and simple one-pot dish.

Serves: 2-4

Time: 1 hour 5 minutes

Ingredients:

For the sauce:

- ¼ cup flour
- ¼ cup butter
- 1 lemon grass stick

- 3 ¼ tablespoons diced onion
- ½ cup heavy cream

Seasoning:

- 4 cups whole milk
- ¼ cup grated gruyere cheese
- 1 cup grated parmesan cheese
- For the lobster:
- 2 ounces' lobster meat
- 1 tablespoon butter
- 1 – 16-ounce pack macaroni

Truffle oil:

- ½ teaspoon ground black pepper
- Truffle slices if desired
- ¼ teaspoon salt

Directions:

1. Dissolve the butter in a heavy based pan, once hot sauté the onions for 3 minutes.

2. Stir in the flour and cook for 3-4 minutes, continue stirring to prevent it from burning, sauce should be white.

3. Slowly add in the milk and keep stirring. As it thickens add more milk.

4. Once all the milk is in, add the lemon grass and cook on low for 10 minutes, keep stirring.

5. Add the cream and cheeses and allow them to dissolve.

6. Correct the seasoning and take off the heat.

7. Heat a pot of salted boiling water and cook the pasta for 8 minutes.

8. Take off and strain the water.

9. Blend together in a pan ½ cup of the sauce with 1 cup of the macaroni.

10. Use a separate pan and add the butter and lobster together and heat until warm.

11. Add the pasta to a serving platter or dish, sprinkle over the truffle oil and fresh truffle if using.

12. Place the meat on top and drizzle over any butter from the pan.

Veal and Roquefort Poutine

A great weeknight meal. Very simple to prepare and delicious to the palate.

Serves: 4

Time: 2 hours 15 minutes

Ingredients:

For the veal:

- 1 leek (roughly chopped)
- 4 pints' veal stock
- 1 clove garlic

- ½ pound veal bones

For the fries:

- 4 cups vegetable oil (for frying)
- ¼ pound Roquefort cheese
- 2 pounds Yukon gold potatoes
- Coarse salt to taste

Directions:

1. To make the gravy, add the leek, bones stock and garlic to a pot and heat.

2. Let simmer for 1 ½ hours, this will allow it to thicken.

3. When done strain the sauce and keep it warm.

4. Meanwhile, peel the potatoes and cut into fries, 3 inches long and 1.4 inch thick.

5. Place them in water and soak for roughly 2 hours to remove the starch.

6. When ready take them out of the water and pat dry.

7. Heat the stove to 150 degrees F.

8. Add the oil to a narrow pot and heat, once the oil is hot, add the fries in batches cooking for 3 minutes, until they become crisp and golden.

9. Remove the unwanted fat and dust with salt.

10. Keep warm in the oven while repeating with the rest.

11. Serve with the gravy and sprinkle with Roquefort cheese over the top.

Ketchup Chip Snack

Canada's favorite chip flavor. A great ketchup snack.

Serves: 4

Time: 23 minutes

Ingredients:

- 2 tablespoons tomato paste
- 2 tablespoons butter or coconut oil
- ½ teaspoon salt

- 2 tablespoons sugar
- 4 teaspoons white vinegar
- ¼ teaspoon garlic powder
- ¼ teaspoon onion powder
- ½ teaspoon smoked paprika
- 12 cups air popped popcorn

Directions:

1. Dissolve the butter using a small pan.

2. Beat in the tomato paste, sugar, vinegar, salt, garlic and onion powders, and paprika. Beat for 60 seconds to dissolve the sugar into the mix.

3. Now take a large bowl and blend the sauce with the popcorn.

4. Heat the stove to 300 degrees F.

5. Lay out the popcorn on parchment paper placed over a baking tray with sides.

6. Bake in the oven for 15-20 minutes, when they become dry to touch take out cool before you snack.

Garlic Fingers with Donair Sauce

Garlic fingers is a must have, especially with Donair sauce; a late night treat.

Serves: 2-4

Time: 30 minutes

Ingredients:

For the sauce:

- ¼ cup white vinegar
- ⅔ cup sweetened condensed milk

- ½ teaspoon garlic powder

For the fingers:

- 1 tablespoon garlic butter, melted
- 1-pound pack pizza dough
- 2 cups grated mozzarella cheese

Directions:

1. Heat the stove to 450 degrees F.

2. Blend together in a bowl the vinegar, condensed milk and garlic powder. Set aside.

3. Take a 15-inch pizza pan and sprinkle cornmeal over it.

4. Place the pizza dough onto a flour dusted work top and roll it out.

5. Once you have a 14-inch round piece, place it on the prepared pan.

6. Smear the garlic over and add the cheese to the top evenly.

7. Cook in the oven for 15 minutes until golden and the cheese has dissolved.

8. Once cooked slice into two, then spin it around with the cut edge at the top and slice into 2-inch fingers.

9. Serve with the sauce.

Maple Sundae

A nice crunchy dessert with a hint of maple syrup and ice-cream.

Serves: 1

Time: 5 minutes

Ingredients:

- 1 tablespoon chopped nuts of your choice
- 3 tablespoons pure maple syrup
- 3 scoops vanilla ice cream

Directions:

1. Add the ice cream to the serving bowl.

2. Spoon the syrup over the ice cream.

3. Dust with the nuts on top.

4. Serve and enjoy.

Canadian Bacon and Vegetable Soup

A perfect meal for those leftover ham from Christmas. Savory, sweet and all in one.

Serves: 8

Time: 1 hour 5 minutes

Ingredients:

- 2 large carrots, diced
- 4 tablespoons olive oil
- 1 ½ cups chopped Canadian bacon
- 2 shallots, diced
- 1 package organic vegetable broth (32-ounce)

- 2 celery stalks, chopped
- 2 tablespoons all-purpose flour
- ¼ cup heavy whipping cream
- 1 medium baking potato, peeled, diced
- ½ teaspoon kosher salt
- ¼ cup chopped parsley
- ½ teaspoon fresh ground black pepper

Directions:

1. Add the oil to large Dutch oven and heat.

2. Once hot, sauté the carrots, shallots and celery for 6-8 minutes until soft.

3. Next, add the bacon and cook for a further 2 minutes.

4. Mix in the flour and after another minute, add the potatoes and broth.

5. Heat until it begins to boil, turn down the heat and cook, simmering for 20 minutes.

6. Once the potatoes are cooked, add the parsley and all the other ingredients.

7. Season to taste and serve.

Canadian Fried Dough Treat

A popular Canadian Winter treat. Sweet, soft and delicious.

Serves: 8

Time: 50 minutes

Ingredients:

- ½ cup warm milk
- ¼ cup warm water
- 2 tablespoons butter (melted)
- 2 ½ teaspoons dried yeast
- 2 tablespoons sugar

- 1 egg
- 2 pints' vegetable oil (for frying)
- ½ teaspoon vanilla
- 2 ½ cups all-purpose flour (plus some for dusting)
- ½ teaspoon salt
- 1 cup sugar (for the topping)
- 1 tablespoon cinnamon for the topping

Directions:

1. Blend together the warm milk, 1 teaspoon sugar, warm water and yeast. Leave combination to ferment for 10 minutes in a large bowl.

2. Next, add in the sugar, vanilla, salt, eggs, and melted butter, combine thoroughly.

3. Now stir in the flour, keep stirring until the dough comes away from the sides of the bowl.

4. Knock it back and knead it until it becomes smooth, this will take around 6 minutes, if it is slightly sticky add a little extra flour.

5. When dough is ready, place into a greased bowl, place a damp cloth over the top, leave on the side to double its size, this will take around 60 minutes.

6. Once again knock it back when ready and cut into 8 pieces of the same size.

7. Place the pieces on a flour dusted worktop and roll into oval shapes, when ready lay them onto a flour dusted baking tray and once again cover them and allow to rise for 30 minutes.

8. Meanwhile, blend together the cinnamon and sugar together in a separate bowl.

9. Add the oil to a pan, this needs to be about 2 inches deep, and heat.

10. Do not let the smoke this will be too hot, if you have a thermometer it should be 350bdegrees F.

11. Place the doughnuts in carefully and cook for 40-60 seconds on either side, take out and pass through the sugar straight away.

12. You can if desired use maple syrup, jam or Nutella.

Canadian Bacon with Maple Syrup

Bacon and maple glaze is a very classy and fashionable dish in the Western Canadian Cuisine.

Serves: 15

Time: 45 minutes

Ingredients:

- 1 tablespoon brown sugar
- ½ cup cider vinegar
- 1 pound Canadian bacon
- ¾ cup maple syrup

Directions:

1. Heat the stove to 300 degrees F.

2. Blend together the syrup, vinegar and sugar using a bowl, then put to one side.

3. Cut the bacon into thick slices, about ½ thick.

4. Lay the slices out on a baking tray and ladle over the syrup.

5. Place in the oven and cook for 30 minutes, take out when ready.

6. As a snack cut into ¼ inch cubes and place on cocktail sticks.

7. Can be eaten as a lunch or dinner for 6 persons.

Maple Fennel Bacon

A classy brunch for all bacon lovers.

Serves: 6

Time: 45 minutes

Ingredients:

- 3 tablespoons maple syrup

- 1 teaspoon fennel seeds
- 12 slices Canadian bacon
- 2 teaspoon brown sugar

Directions:

1. Heat the stove to 375 degrees F.

2. Place tin foil over a baking tray and set a rack on top of it.

3. Lay the bacon over the rack, you can slightly overlap them but not too much.

4. Blend together the sugar and syrup in a bowl, now smear it over the bacon.

5. Dust the bacon with the seeds and black pepper.

6. Cook in the middle of the oven for 25 -35 minutes.

7. Remove when cooked and golden brown, rest on the side for 5 minutes and enjoy.

Conclusion

Thank you for sticking with us all the way the end of this Canadian Cookbook with us. We hope you enjoyed all 30 delicious Canadian recipes that are perfect for any time of day.

So, what happens next?

Nothing breathes perfection like practice. So, keep on cooking and enjoying new and exciting meals with your whole family. Then whenever you are ready for another spark of delicious inspiration grab another one of our books and let us continue your culinary journey together.

Remember, drop us a review if you loved what you read and until we meet again, keep on cooking delicious food.

Manufactured by Amazon.ca
Bolton, ON